STRETCHY
LIBRARY LESSONS

RESEARCH SKILLS

Pat Miller

Fort Atkinson, Wisconsin

For Bonnie Miller,
soft hearted, tough minded—my favorite adventuress.

Published by UpstartBooks
W5527 Highway 106
P.O. Box 800
Fort Atkinson, Wisconsin 53538-0800
1-800-448-4887

Copyright © 2003 by Pat Miller

Contents

Introduction

In my 16 years as a school librarian, I have worked in three elementary libraries. None of them have had the same schedule, and they were probably all different from the one you have. In talking with library media specialists from across the country, I've discovered that the fixed schedule is very much a staple, despite the research and standards that urge "point of need" flexible library usage and scheduling.

Some school librarians have 45-minute classes, some only 30 minutes and some have a full hour. Class length even varies at the same school based on grade level, school events and school population. It also depends on whether or not librarians are part of "the rotation." If they are, the library serves as a class that students attend so teachers can have planning time.

The Stretchy Library Lessons series is designed to give you ideas for adapting lessons to fit your time constraints. Though the lessons are based on standards, they do not constitute a curriculum. Though they cross the elementary grade levels, they do not comprise enough lessons to get you through a semester. Instead, Stretchy Library Lessons gives you a variety of ways to pack a lot of learning into each lesson and to extend a short lesson with related games, Web sites, activities and other reading material.

How to Use This Book

Stretchy Library Lessons: Research Skills has 10 basic lessons and 10 stretchy lessons. All of the lessons are designed to appeal to multiple intelligences, learning styles and reading abilities. The skills index on page 7 correlates each lesson by grade level and skill.

Each Stretchy Library Lesson includes:

- **Research Skills.** These are taken from overlapping documents at the state and national level for English Language Arts.

- **A Range of Grades.** The lessons are K–5, though they can be adapted for preschoolers, special needs students and sixth graders.

- **A Purpose.** This helps library media specialists integrate the lessons with class curriculum, district and state media literacy standards and social and emotional goals.

- **Prerequisite Skills.** Research skills can't be thoroughly taught in a single 20- or even 60-minute class. The lessons in this book should follow an introduction of the research skills needed for the lesson.

- **The Format.** Listing the format (game, contest, read-aloud, etc.) helps you appeal to different learning styles.

- **A List of Materials.** These are readily available or easily made and should be gathered before you teach the lesson.

- **Items to Prepare in Advance.** If you teach all grades each day as I do, your lesson materials need to be well organized because there is little time between classes. This section tells you what needs to be made, purchased or found before a class comes in.

- **Twenty-Minute Activity.** My schedule is fixed at 30-minute intervals, with a few bands of flexible time that can be scheduled by any teacher. Allowing 10 minutes for students to select books, I try to design my basic class lesson to fit a 20-minute session. Most of the main activities can be taught in 20 minutes. The activities include all forms, worksheets and patterns that you will need.

- **The Stretchy Activity.** This activity extends the lesson to fit a longer time frame. If you have short classes like I do, the lessons in this book may be enough for 20 sessions. The stretchy activities include their own materials list, items to prepare in advance and steps for teaching the lesson.

- **Resources.** The books can be used instead of the featured title or as an extension. I tried to include newer works, all of which are in print and available from bookstores or on-line at press time. Always put these or similar books on display near your teaching area in case a teacher or child wants to extend their learning. I've also included some professional resources that cover a particular research skill more thoroughly. The Web sites are current as of this printing, but if you get an error message, perform a keyword search on the Web site title. Be sure the title is enclosed in quotation marks.

Key Research Skills

1. Use pictures and print to gather information.

2. Use alphabetical order to locate information.

3. Use a strategy to form questions and locate answers.

4. Use the library catalog to locate reading and research materials.

5. Use the table of contents, guide words, index and key words to find information.

6. Interpret and/or represent information using outlines, timelines, pictures, map coordinates, charts and graphs.

7. Use dictionaries, atlases, thesauri, almanacs and encyclopedias to locate information.

8. Use reference and nonfiction computer programs to locate information.

9. Summarize and organize by taking notes or outlining.

10. Acquire information from on-line resources.

Grade Appropriate Skills Index

Twenty-minute activities are in bold.

LESSON TITLE	GRADES							SKILLS									
	K	1	2	3	4	5		1	2	3	4	5	6	7	8	9	10
Sticks and Stones (ABC order)	X	X	X	X	X	X			X								
Alphabetical Author	X	X	X	X	X	X			X								
Partner Passports to PAC				X	X	X		X	X		X					X	X
Seek and Find				X	X	X		X	X	X	X					X	X
Strategic Puppets (Big 6™)				X	X	X				X	X		X			X	X
Puppet Museum	X	X	X	X	X	X		X					X				
Famous Folks (e-Resources)				X	X	X		X		X	X			X	X		X
A Place in History				X	X	X		X					X				
Take Note!	X	X	X	X	X	X		X		X					X	X	
Prepare to Speak	X	X	X	X	X	X		X				X					
Using the Index				X	X	X		X	X			X	X	X		X	
Index Questions				X	X	X		X		X			X				
Dictionary Go Fish	X	X	X	X	X	X		X	X	X		X		X			
Dictionary Dive	X	X	X	X	X	X		X	X	X		X		X			
The Great Race (Atlas)				X	X	X			X				X	X			
Where in the World am I?				X	X	X		X	X			X	X	X			
Taming Tired Tales (Thesaurus)				X	X	X			X			X		X			X
Thesaurus Triumph				X	X	X			X			X		X			X
Almanac Jeopardy				X	X	X		X	X	X		X	X	X	X		X
Almanac Scavenge				X	X	X		X	X	X		X	X		X		X

Sticks and Stones

(ABC Order)

Research Skills: To use alphabetical order to locate information.

Grades: K–1 (single letter), 2–5 (two letters), 3–5 (three letters)

Purpose: To use alphabetical order to locate information and relate it to the author's names in the library.

Prerequisite Skills: Knowledge of alphabetical order and how it is used in the library (to shelve books by author's last name, file library cards by last name and look up entries in on-line and text references).

Format: Tactile Activity

Materials:

- 6 sets of tagboard squares or white or gray polished river stones (available at craft stores) for each grade level (26 per set)

- 6 scts of craft sticks or tongue depressors for each grade level (17 per set for K–1, 34 per set for 2–5, 51 per set for 3–5)

- plastic bag or envelope for each set

- permanent markers

Prepare in Advance: Prepare the sets of "sticks and stones." For each set, make 26 stones. With a permanent marker, write a single letter on each tagboard square or stone. The letters A–L should be in one color and the letters M–Z in another color. If desired, draw a stone shape on each piece of tagboard. On the sticks, write each of the author's names from pages 12–13, depending on the grade level. The A–L authors should match the color of the A–L stones. Do the same for the M–Z authors. Place each set of sticks and stones in the plastic bag or envelope.

Activity Directions:

1. Form the class into teams of four. Each team should have two pairs of students.

2. Give each team a set of sticks and stones. The team should pour them onto a work area and divide the sticks and stones by color into two groups.

3. Each pair of students should take a color group. They should arrange the stones in alphabetical order, from top to bottom.

4. To the right of the stones they should organize the author sticks. Depending on the level, there will be one, two or three sticks per stone (not all stones, like "q" and "z," will have authors).

5. Remind the students that the sticks are arranged by the author's LAST name. If there is more than one stick per stone, than the sticks should also be in alphabetical order.

6. After all of the sticks are arranged, use the lists on pages 12–13 to call out the author names so the students can check their work. If necessary, students can correct the order as you give the answer.

Alphabetical Author

Materials:

- sticks from the previous activity

- large can

- bookmarks *(optional)*

Activity Directions:

1. Have the students randomly choose one of the author sticks from the can.

2. The students should use their stick to locate the author and choose a book. You may want to have them check with you before searching so you can tell them if their author writes picture book fiction or chapter book fiction. The students should locate the book by the author's last name without assistance.

3. When they show you their find, they can exchange the stick for a bookmark.

Resources

Books:

You might want to share some of the creative alphabet books that are available on all different topics. A few to begin with are:

<u>For younger readers:</u>

ABCD: An Alphabet Book of Cats and Dogs by Shelia Moxley. Little, Brown, 2001. Photographs of dogs and cats participate in alliterative adventures like "Freddie fishes for flounder."

Alphabet Under Construction by Denise Fleming. Henry Holt, 2002. This is an action alphabet, with a mouse folding the "F," measuring the "M," etc.

Picture a Letter by Brad Sneed. Penguin Putnam, 2002. This wordless alphabet book will fascinate even adults as the reader searches for people, objects and animals hidden in the pictures.

<u>For older students</u>:

The Valley of the Golden Mummies by Joan Holub. Penguin Putnam, 2002. Alphabetically, students will learn facts about Egyptians and their ancient burial traditions.

The Young Adventurer's Guide to Everest: From Avalanche to Zopkiok by Jonathan Chester. Ten Speed Press, 2002. This alphabet book provides color photographs with information about mountaineering on Mt. Everest.

Web sites:

ABC Order
www.learningplanet.com/act/abcorder.asp
An interactive game with sound and animation asks children to supply the missing letter in a sequence of three. Game is from A to I. For a complete version, and access to a dozen more alphabet and ordering games (as well as a wealth of other activities), a paid subscription to LearningPlanet.com is required.

Alphabet Zoo
www.primarygames.com/ABC%20Zoo/start.htm
An animated game that asks children to put groups of three animals in alphabetical order.

The Alphabuddies
www.dltk-kids.com/alphabuddies/index.html
Includes ABC worksheets for tracing or coloring, alphabet templates for puppets or flash cards and numerous activities and crafts based on the alphabet.

"Sticks and Stones" Authors

Set 1: (Grades K–1)

Match the author to the first letter of the last name. Not all of the letters have a matching author.

A	Tedd Arnold
B	Molly Bang
C	Donald Crews
D	Niki Daly
E	Lois Ehlert
F	Jules Feiffer
G	Jack Gantos
H	Eric Hill
J	Ann Jonas
K	Ezra Jack Keats
L	Leo Lionni
M	Bill Martin
O	Helen Oxenbury
R	Phyllis Root
S	Maurice Sendak
T	Nancy Tafuri
W	Rosemary Wells

Set 2: (Grades 2–5)

Order the authors by the first two letters of the last name. Not all of the letters have a matching author.

A	Harry Allard, George Ancona
B	Norman Bridwell, Eve Bunting
C	Eric Carle, Joanna Cole
D	Judy Delton, Diane Dillon
F	Mem Fox, Don Freeman
G	Paul Goble, Eloise Greenfield

H	Russell Hoban, Pat Hutchins
K	Steven Kellogg, Eric Kimmel
L	Loreen Leedy, Arnold Lobel
M	David McPhail, Mercer Meyer
N	W. Nikola-Lisa, Laura Joffe Numeroff
P	Jerry Pinkney, Patricia Polacco
R	H. A. Rey, Cynthia Rylant
S	Richard Scarry, Dr. Seuss
T	Simms Taback, Mark Teague
V	Chris Van Allsburg, Judith Viorst
W	Kate Waters, David Wiesner

Set 3: (Grades 3–5)

Order the authors by the first three letters of the last name. Not all of the letters have a matching author.

A	Lloyd Alexander, K. A. Applegate, Avi
B	Jan Brett, Marc Brown, Betsy Byars
C	Beverly Cleary, Pam Conrad, Bruce Coville
D	Roald Dahl, Paula Danziger, Bruce Degen
F	Sid Fleischman, Russell Freedman, Jean Fritz
G	Jean Craighead George, Shelley Gill, Dan Gutman
H	Virginia Hamilton, Will Hobbs, Lee Bennett Hopkins
K	Helen Ketteman, E. L. Konigsburg, Gordon Korman
L	Lois Lenski, C. S. Lewis, Lois Lowry
M	Patricia MacLachlan, Ann Martin, Patricia McKissack
N	Phyllis Reynolds Naylor, Garth Nix, Joan Lowery Nixon
P	Katherine Paterson, Gary Paulsen, Richard Peck
R	Wilson Rawls, Barbara Robinson, J. K. Rowling
S	Jon Scieszka, William Steig, R. L. Stine
T	Marvin Terban, Mike Thaler, J. R. R. Tolkien
W	Bill Wallace, Laura Ingalls Wilder, David Wisniewski
Y	Tammy Yee, Jane Yolen, Ed Young

Partner Passports to PAC

Research Skills: To use pictures and print to gather information, alphabetical order to locate information and the library catalog to locate reading and research materials. To summarize and organize by taking notes or outlining and to acquire information from on-line resources.

Grades: 3–5

Purpose: To review locating a book by title, author or subject; to put a book on hold; and to review looking up students' records (any additional purposes specific to your automated system).

Prerequisite Skills: Beginning knowledge of searching by title, author or keyword; how to put items on hold; and how to look up students' circulation records.

Format: Student Brochure

Materials:

- PAC Passport for each student (see page 17)

- PAC stations

- pencils

- PAC Ready Reference chart (sample on page 15) for each PAC station

- stickers *(optional)*

Prepare in Advance: Write your school name in columns 1 and 4 of the Passport. Make any necessary changes so the Passport agrees with your PAC. Check that all of the items can be found in your library. Photocopy enough PAC Passports for your class. Cut them out, then fold them into brochures by folding the paper in half with the printing on the inside, then folding the top edge back towards the fold and the bottom edge back towards the fold to make an accordion.

Be sure all of the computers are on and have the PAC up on the screen. Provide pencils next to each computer. Add a book to your catalog called "Fictitious Title" so that all students can "reserve" it. After classes are complete, delete the fictitious book and all of its holds.

Modify the PAC Ready Reference chart to fit your procedures and automated catalog. Then photocopy or re-create it. Make enough charts for each PAC station. Mount it on the side of the monitor at each station.

PAC Ready Reference	
What I Know	**What Search I Use**
I know the author	Author Keyword
I know the title	Title Keyword
I know the subject	Subject Keyword
I know my account number	My Library Account

Note: Modify this chart to fit the PAC for your automated circulation program.

Activity Directions:

1. In groups of two, have students access the PAC and complete the 10 questions in the brochure. Passports are earned in pairs, with one student answering the odd question and the other student the even question. Both students need to write the answers in their passport.

2. After each question, the students raise their hands to be checked by the teacher or librarian. If the answer is correct, they receive a sticker or initial in the "Customs Check" box. If the answer is incorrect, they receive assistance and a review.

3. After all 10 stickers or signatures are earned, students earn their Passport to the Library. Provide a special sticker or rubber stamp for the last page.

Seek and Find

Materials:

- PAC stations

- paper

- pencil for each student

Prepare in Advance: Provide paper and a pencil for each student.

Activity Directions:

1. Have the students write the name of one of their favorite authors, their favorite book and a subject that interests them.

2. At the PAC computers, the students should locate a book for each of their choices. Have them show you the appropriate screen so you can initial their paper. When the students have three initials, they earn a special bookmark or an extra book to check out.

Resources

Books:

How to be School Smart: Super Study Skills by Elizabeth James and Carol Barkin. William Morrow & Co., 1998. Two of the chapters are Searching the Library and Searching the Internet.

Skills for Life: Information Literacy for Grades K–6 by Christine Allen. Linworth, 2002.

Web site:

Gateway to Library Catalogs
www.loc.gov/z3950
Search the Library of Congress catalog or hundreds of others arranged by alphabetical order. Libraries include public, college and university and institutes.

PAC PASSPORT

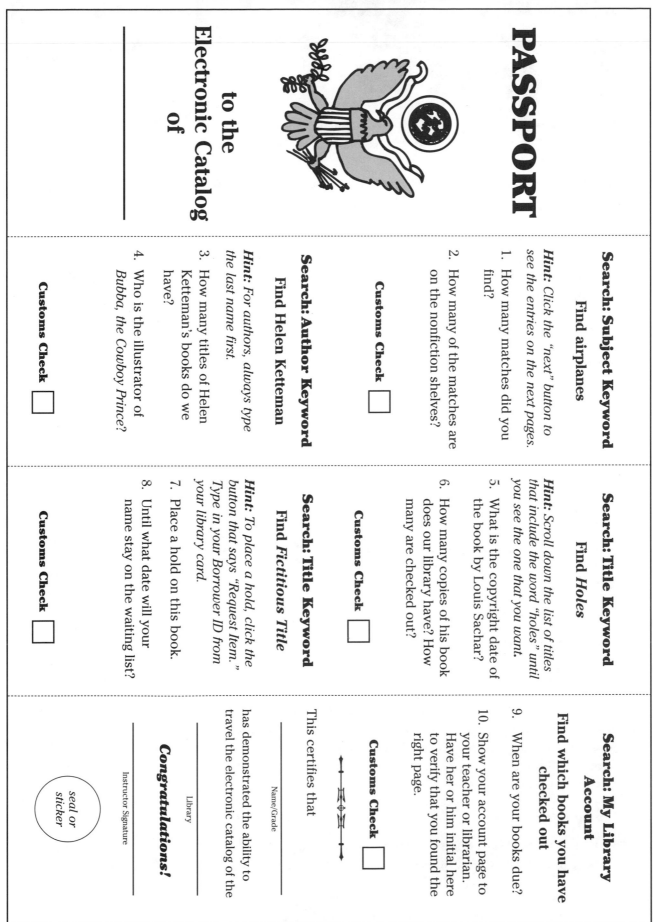

PASSPORT

to the
Electronic Catalog
of

_____

Search: Subject Keyword
Find airplanes

Hint: Click the "next" button to see the entries on the next pages.

1. How many matches did you find?

2. How many of the matches are on the nonfiction shelves?

Customs Check ☐

Search: Author Keyword
Find Helen Ketteman

Hint: For authors, always type the last name first.

3. How many titles of Helen Ketteman's books do we have?

4. Who is the illustrator of *Bubba, the Cowboy Prince?*

Customs Check ☐

Search: Title Keyword
Find *Holes*

Hint: Scroll down the list of titles that include the word "holes" until you see the one that you want.

5. What is the copyright date of the book by Louis Sachar?

6. How many copies of his book does our library have? How many are checked out?

Customs Check ☐

Search: Title Keyword
Find *Fictitious Title*

Hint: To place a hold, click the button that says "Request Item." Type in your Borrower ID from your library card.

7. Place a hold on this book.

8. Until what date will your name stay on the waiting list?

Customs Check ☐

Search: My Library Account
Find which books you have checked out

9. When are your books due?

10. Show your account page to your teacher or librarian. Have her or him initial here to verify that you found the right page.

Customs Check ☐

This certifies that

_____
Name/Grade

has demonstrated the ability to travel the electronic catalog of the

_____
Library

Congratulations!

_____
Instructor Signature

(seal or sticker)

Strategic Puppets

(Big 6™)

This lesson works best as part of a cooperative unit with a teacher who is teaching a folklore or fairy tale unit.

Research Skills: To use a strategy to form questions and locate answers and the library catalog to locate reading and research materials. To interpret and/or represent information using outlines; summarize and organize by taking notes or outlining; and acquire information from on-line resources.

Grades: 3–5

Purpose: To organize a puppet project using an information strategy like Big 6™, I-Search, FLIP-It or other method to accompany a curriculum unit. This can also be the culmination activity of a "how-to" unit.

Prerequisite Skills: Familiarity with the Information Seeking Strategy used at your school.

Format: Fairy Tale Puppets

Materials:

- puppet slides and projector or PowerPoint of puppet pictures

- overhead and screen

- transparency film and pen

- How to Make a Puppet Worksheet (see page 21) for each student

- Puppet Planning Form (see page 22) for each student

Prepare in Advance: Scan pictures (or take slides) of simple puppets you want the students to make. You can make the puppets yourself and photograph them or scan photos from various puppet books. If you use books, be sure to give credit for each photo. Organize and insert slides into the carousel or a PowerPoint presentation. Make photocopies of the worksheet and form for each student.

Activity Directions:

1. Have students select a fairy tale or folktale from the library to read. Let them know that they will be making a puppet of the main character.

2. Show the students your slide show or PowerPoint presentation to see the various types of puppets they can make.

3. Have the students choose the type of puppet they want to make. They should consider what type of puppet best fits their character as well as the materials needed and the time involved in making the puppets. Provide puppet-making books and/or Web sites to examine in the library (see Resources on page 20).

4. Dedicate several class and/or library periods to completing the research and creating the puppets. Have students document the resources they used for making their puppets.

5. Assign a deadline for the puppets to be completed.

Puppet Museum

Once the puppets are finished, the library media specialist can furnish the display space to create a Puppet Museum for the entire school to see.

Grades: K–5

Materials:

- tent cards and pens

- tables or cabinet tops to display the puppets

- signs to identify parts of the museum display

- digital camera or camera with slide film

Prepare in Advance: Students should bring their completed puppets to the library along with the book that the character comes from.

Activity Directions:

1. Give each student a tent card. Have them write the name of the character, the book title and their name on the card.

2. Have the students separate the puppets into categories according to how they are made. The categories might include: stick, hand, box, finger, recycled (made from sponges, kitchen spoons, etc.), shadow, sock, glove, envelope, etc. Display a large decorated sign for each type of puppet.

3. Set up each puppet with its accompanying book and tent card.

4. Have the students make invitations to send to the classes, parents and administrators.

5. Include an announcement in the library newsletter or local newspaper with a picture or two. Take pictures of all of the puppets to be used in next year's slide show or PowerPoint presentation. Include a slide that gives credit to all creators.

Resources

Books:

Fractured Fairy Tales: Puppet Plays & Patterns by Marilyn Lohnes. Upstart Books, 2002.

The Muppets Make Puppets! by Cheryl Henson, et al. Workman Publishing Company, 1994.

Puppet and Theater Activities: Theatrical Things to Do and Make edited by Beth Murray. Boyds Mills Press, 1994.

Puppets by Meryl Doney. Franklin Watts, 1996.

Simple Puppets from Everyday Materials by Barbara MacDonald Buetter. Sterling Publishing Company, 1998.

Storytelling with Puppets by Connie Champlin. American Library Association, 1997.

Teaching Information and Technology Skills: The Big 6 in Elementary Schools by Michael B. Eisenberg and Robert E. Berkowitz. Linworth, 1999.

The Usborne Book of Puppets by Ken Haines and Gill Harvery. EDCP, 1998.

Web sites:

Family Fun: All About Puppets
familyfun.go.com/crafts/buildmodel/specialfeature/
puppets_crafts_sf/
Directions for making dozens of different puppets and links to other puppetry sites.

Puppeteers of America
www.puppeteers.org
Find lots of assistance from professional puppeteers and links to more puppetry sites, including ones that show how to make various puppets.

Name _____   Date _____

How to Make a Puppet

Name of fairy tale and character: _____

_____

Type of puppet: _____

Materials needed: _____

_____

_____

_____

_____

_____

_____

Directions: Write specific directions for making your puppet (use the back if needed).
Make sure you can follow the directions.

_____

_____

_____

_____

_____

_____

_____

_____

_____

_____

_____

Name _____   Teacher _____

Puppet Planning Form

1. What is the assignment? _____

   _____

2. What possible resources can I use? _____

   _____

   _____

3. How will I make my puppet? _____

   _____

   _____

   _____

   _____

4. How will I present my puppet to the class? _____

   _____

   _____

5. Did I complete the assignment? _____

   Did I do a good job on the project? _____

   If I did this again, what would I do differently? _____

   _____

   _____

   _____

   _____

   _____

Famous Folks

(e-Resources)

Research Skills: To use pictures and print to gather information, a strategy to form questions and locate answers, a library catalog to locate reading and research materials, an encyclopedia and CD resources to locate information and on-line resources to acquire information.

Grades: 3–5

Purpose: To use electronic resources to locate needed information.

Prerequisite Skills: The ability to open bookmarked sites and navigate a CD-ROM.

Format: Computer Activity

Materials:

- Fact Finding Sheet (see page 26)

- Internet Search Plan forms (see page 27)

- computers with bookmarked sites

- an appropriate encyclopedia on CD-ROM or an encyclopedia Web site

- related biography books

Prepare in Advance: Make copies of the Fact Finding Sheet for each student. Photocopy the Internet Search Plan onto colored card stock and cut it to size. Display related biography books. Load the encyclopedia CD-ROM on computers and bookmark the following sites:

Biography.com
www.biography.com
Contains over 15,000 short biographical entries. Have students use the BioSearch window at the top left of the page. Enter the name with last name first.

Yahooligans Biographies Directory
www.yahooligans.com/school_bell/social_studies/history/biographies
Includes lists of biographies by country; pictures; speeches and videos; and sites grouped by royals, athletes, explorers, women, etc. All sites listed are appropriate for children. Search by clicking on the appropriate part of the directory or by typing the name into the search window on the main page.

Activity Directions:

1. Teach the students to use the Internet Search Plan. I use this when students come in to the library to use the computers independently. They must complete the card and have me initial it before they can use the Internet to search.

2. Have the students choose a famous person and formulate questions that they would like to find out about the person. Then have them use the bookmarked sites to answer their questions. Have them record the information on their Fact Finding Sheet.

3. The students should continue to verify previous information on their fact sheet and add to it by checking the on-line or CD-ROM encyclopedia and an appropriate biography of the person.

4. Have the students use the information to create a report about the famous person in a format selected by the teacher. The report might be given while dressed as the person, presented in PowerPoint or any other creative method.

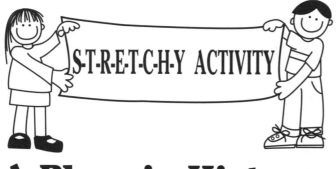

A Place in History

Materials:

- a person outline for each student (see page 28)

- a length of clothesline and tiny clothespins (available at hobby or craft stores)

- pushpins

- index cards

- crayons

- scrap paper

- scissors

- white paper

- pencils for each student or enough to share

- three-ring binder *(optional)*

Prepare in Advance: Tack the pushpins along a straight line into a large bulletin board or empty wall. String the clothesline over the pushpins so it doesn't sag. Use the index cards to make a card for each decade from 1750 to the present. If needed, more cards can be made as students clip their people to the timeline. Photocopy a person outline for each student and gather the remaining supplies.

Activity Directions:

1. Have the students use the crayons and scrap paper to add appropriate clothing to their person, as well as shoes, hair and any items held in their hands.

2. Add the person's name and years of birth and death in the label at the feet. Cut the person out.

3. Use the birth year to add the person to the timeline. If two people have the same birth year, put them in order by their birth date (this should be in the student's report). After all of the pictures are mounted, hang the appropriate decade cards over the first person from that decade.

4. If desired, bind the completed reports into a three-hole binder that can be available for other students to examine or check out of the library.

Resources

Books:

Biography for Beginners: Sketches for Early Readers. Issue 2, Winter 2002. Favorable Impressions. This is a bi-annual subscription that provides eight biographical profiles in each volume for readers ages six to nine. Back issues can be ordered as well.

I-Search, You Search, We All Learn to Research: A How-to-Do-It Manual for Teaching Elementary School Students to Solve Information Problems by Donna Duncan and Laura Lockhart. Neal-Schuman Publishers, 2000.

Web sites:

Surfing for ABC's
www.siec.k12.in.us/~west/proj/abc
Kindergarteners and first graders created this site by using the Yahooligans search engine to find suitable Web sites for every letter of the alphabet. Lesson plan for the project is included.

Teacher's Guide: Teaching Internet Literacy: Student Activities
www.yahooligans.com/tg/activities.html
Includes teacher plans and links to do Web Site Comparisons (including some bogus sites), Compare Information to Non-Internet Sources, Create and Manipulate Information, How to Learn More About a Site, Compare Two Sources and Professional vs. Amateur Coverage.

Name _____

Topic _____

Fact Finding Sheet

My Questions	My Answers	My Sources
		Book _____ Encyclopedia _____ Web site _____ Title/address: _____ Author: _____ Copyright: _____
		Book _____ Encyclopedia _____ Web site _____ Title/address: _____ Author: _____ Copyright: _____
		Book _____ Encyclopedia _____ Web site _____ Title/address: _____ Author: _____ Copyright: _____

Internet Search Plan Forms

Internet Search Plan

Name: _____

Teacher: _____ **Librarian Approval:** _____

Web Address or Question: _____

_____

_____

Search Terms: _____

_____

Internet Search Plan

Name: _____

Teacher: _____ **Librarian Approval:** _____

Web Address or Question: _____

_____

_____

Search Terms: _____

_____

Famous Person Outline

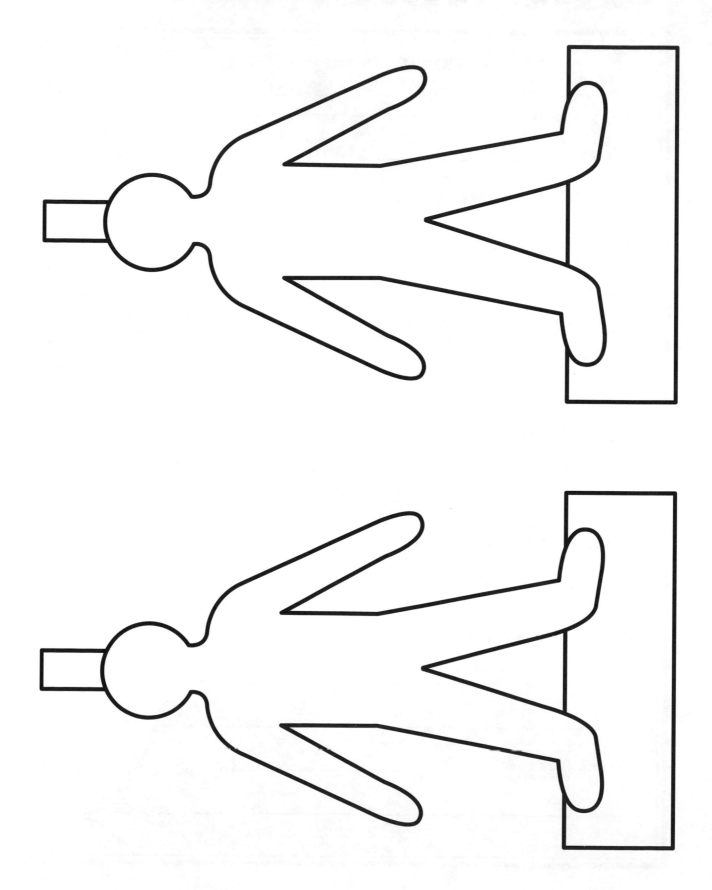

Take Note!

Research Skills: To use pictures and print to gather information; form questions and locate answers; use computer programs to locate information; and summarize and organize by taking notes.

Grades: K–2 Listening Activity; 3–5 Research Activity

Purpose: To locate answers to questions. In primary grades, the questions will be established before hearing the story and answered after the story as a group. In intermediate grades, questions will pertain to a topic, then used to make a three-minute speech. Students also use an index to locate helpful parts of book.

Prerequisite Skills: For K–2, experience with summarizing information and adding information to a chart. For 3–5, knowledge of an Information Search Strategy (like Big 6™) and how to locate the information needed in the Animal Research Bank, Native American Research Bank, Famous Person Research Bank (see pages 37–42) or other topics pertinent to the curriculum. Students should know how to use an index to locate helpful parts of a book. (See Using the Index on page 43.)

Format: Tactile Activity

Materials:

For K–2:

- a transparency and washable marking pen for each class

- copy of *Mrs. Katz and Tush* by Patricia Polacco or other titles that include cultural and bilingual information

For 3–5:

- Students should bring their notes from a previous fact search. This activity includes an example of the completed Animal Research Bank (see pages 35–36) and notes from the book *Cockroaches* by Larry Dane Brimner (see page 34).

- research sources for students including books, encyclopedias, Internet sites and CD-ROM programs on animals, Native Americans, famous Americans, etc.

- photocopy the Animal Research Bank, Native American Research Bank and Famous Person Research Bank forms (see pages 37–42) or other pertinent topic

Prepare in Advance:

For K–2:

Divide the transparency into three areas horizontally. Write the title and author at the top. Label the sections "words," "foods" and "customs." (See sample form and answers on page 33.)

Make a transparency of page 34 and of the sample notes on pages 35 and 36. Copy by hand the demonstration notes (see example on page 34) onto a 3" x 5" note card. The circled words are technical words to refer back to during the lesson. Have the forms for Native Americans, Animals and Famous People available for students to choose from.

Activity Directions:

For K–2:

1. Tell the students that much can be learned from nonfiction and even fiction books. In *Mrs. Katz and Tush,* we find out about a friend that Patricia Polacco had as a child. Ms. Polacco is Jewish and includes many words, foods and traditions from her faith and former homeland of Russia.

2. Show the blank transparency, "Mrs. Katz and Tush Fact Bank," and tell the students that we are going to learn from Mrs. Katz, just as Patricia did when she was a child. When students hear a word, food or custom that sounds new to them, they should raise their hand so it can be added to the fact bank.

3. Read the book carefully and with lots of expression. Stop at the right points if children don't and add the words to your sheet. Students will get the idea and listen more carefully after they see what you are doing.

4. At the end of the book, review all of the new things learned from the book.

For 3–5:

1. Briefly show students the three resources you used for your report—the book, encyclopedia and Internet site. (See sources on page 36.)

2. Display the transparency of the notes you took from these three sources. Explain the abbreviations to the students and note other ways that the notes were shortened. Comment on why some words are circled (technical terms).

3. Point out how you did the bibliography and refer to it in each note section.

4. Show the actual hand-written card. Then show the note card transparency so students can see what's condensed on the card.

5. Have the students choose what they would like to research, then pick up a form. They can spend the rest of the class time researching.

Note: You can also use these forms as a model for other topics assigned by teachers.

Prepare to Speak

Materials:

For 3–5:

• note card from previous lesson

Prepare in Advance:

For K–2:

Another title that includes cultural and bilingual information, perhaps from Pat Mora (see Bibliography on page 77) or the transparency from the previous lesson.

For 3–5:

Practice your speech based on the sources you read and the notes you took, especially the note card, so you can deliver a good three-minute example for the students.

Activity Directions:

For K–2:

To extend the activity, read another book and repeat the steps. Or use the information that the class gathered on the transparency to have the students help you write a story about "The Customs of Mrs. Katz."

For 3–5:

1. Give a three-minute speech based on the notes you took.

2. Have the students prepare and give their own speeches based on the notes they took in the previous lesson.

Resources

Books:

How to Write Super School Reports by Elizabeth James and Carol Barkin. HarperCollins, 1998. Explains how to find and organize information, how to take notes and cite sources and how to write and revise the final version.

Practical Steps to the Research Process for Elementary School by Deborah B. Stanley. Greenwood, 2001. Part of the Information Literacy series.

Turning Kids on to Research: The Power of Motivation by Ruth V. Small and Marilyn P. Arnone. Greenwood, 2000.

Web sites:

Ideas About Note Taking and Citing Sources
www.big6.com/showarticle.php?id=78

World History and Geography: A Guide for High School Teachers
www.studentsfriend.com
This was written for high school, but contains many basic instructions and forms that can be used by upper elementary as well. Partial contents include: Note Card Models, Guide to Outlines and Guide to Report Writing and Evaluation Forms.

Mrs. Katz and Tush Fact Bank
Sample Transparency

Words	Foods	Customs
tush: bottom	lamb	Kept dairy and meat on separate dishes (kosher).
bubee: grandmother	chicken	
kaddish: memorial service	matzoh	Said prayers and put a stone on the tombstone (kaddish).
kugel: coffee cake	kugel	
matzoh: unleavened bread	gefilte fish	Celebrated Passover with bitter herbs, lamb, gefilte fish, chicken and potato pancakes.
bubeleh: baby	spiced apples	
kitteleh: kitty	potato pancakes	Married under a huppa.
mazel tov: good luck		
kosher: meals that have been prepared according to strict dietary laws		
seder: ("order") the ritualistic meal that commemorates the Passover and the Jews' flight from Egypt		
huppa: a canopy held over a couple getting married		
Yiddish: everyday Jewish language		
shalom: peace be with you		

Sample Note Cards for Transparency

Note Card—Front Side

compound eyes–most of head, sees in all direc.

(carapace)–skeleton on outside like armor

3 body parts (head, abdomen, thorax) 2 pr. wings, rarely flies

runs 3 mph

6 hairy legs, claws   cerci–back sensors

sensors in leg joints automatically move legs when motion sensed

live anywhere there's water, not Arctic -- only 1% live with humans

nearly 3,700 kinds

(omnivore)–eats anything   egg case–48 babies called nymphs

young molt 6 to 12 times before full-grown

Note Card—Back Side

living fossils   been around 350 million years (even before dinos)
blood is clear

can hold breath 40 min.

can live w/out brain

live 1 week w/out head -- dies of thirst

breathes through spiracles, 4 on thorax, 8 on abdomen

would be the one animal that could survive any catastrophe,
    including nuclear, because it is so hardy and adaptable

Sample Animal Research Bank

What does your animal look like?

Source: book __X__   encyclopedia __X__   Internet site _____

compound eyes, use wings more like parachute

feelers—smell, taste, feel   (carapace)—skeleton on outside like armor

3 body parts: head, thorax, abdomen

eyes cover most of its head—sees all directions at once

6 legs covered with hairs

2 claws at end of each leg hold on to any surface

2 pairs of wings, rarely fly, run instead

2 (cerci) at back sense vibrations
leg joints automatically move with vibration—either sound, air or motion

What is its food and habitat?

Source: book __X__   encyclopedia __X__   Internet site _____

some Asian cockroaches—entirely amphibious (swim)

1% live with humans

live anywhere it's damp, mostly outside

TX mostly has the small one called German roach

found in every habitat except Arctic

food: (omnivore) eats plants, meat, other roaches, cloth, paper, even plastic—eats nearly everything!

Sample Animal Research Bank (continued)

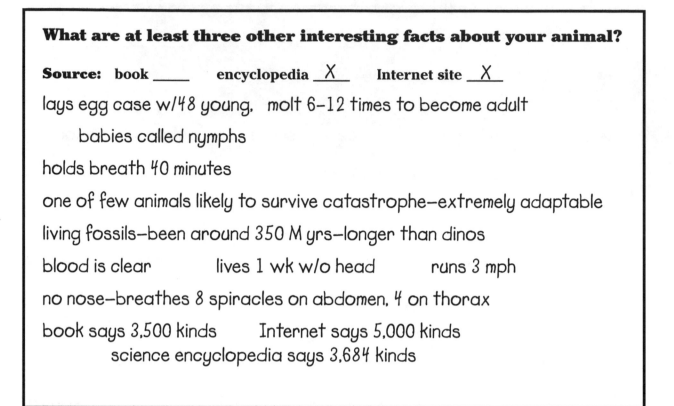

What are at least three other interesting facts about your animal?

Source: book _____ encyclopedia _X_ Internet site _X_

lays egg case w/48 young, molt 6–12 times to become adult

    babies called nymphs

holds breath 40 minutes

one of few animals likely to survive catastrophe–extremely adaptable

living fossils–been around 350 M yrs–longer than dinos

blood is clear   lives 1 wk w/o head   runs 3 mph

no nose–breathes 8 spiracles on abdomen, 4 on thorax

book says 3,500 kinds   Internet says 5,000 kinds

         science encyclopedia says 3,684 kinds

Animal Bibliography

Book

Title: True Book of Cockroaches

Author: Larry Dane Brimner

Encyclopedia

Title: Illustrated Encyclopedia of Wildlife

Volume: 12   **Page(s):** 2389–2394

Internet Site

Title: "Yucky Roach World: Roaches Revealed"

Address: http://yucky.kids.discovery.com/flash/roaches

Copyright: Discovery Communications, Inc., 2000

Name _____   Animal _____

Animal Research Bank

What does your animal look like?

Source: book _____   encyclopedia _____   Internet site _____

What is its food and habitat?

Source: book _____   encyclopedia _____   Internet site _____

Animal Research Bank (continued)

What are at least three other interesting facts about your animal?

Source: book _____   encyclopedia _____   Internet site _____

Animal Bibliography

Book
Title: _____

Author: _____

Encyclopedia
Title: _____

Volume: _____   Page(s): _____

Internet Site
Title: _____

Address: _____

Copyright: _____

Native American Research Bank

What kind of clothing and food did your tribe use and how were they obtained?

Source: book _____ encyclopedia _____ Internet site _____

Where was this tribe located? Where is it today?

Source: book _____ encyclopedia _____ Internet site _____

What are three other interesting things about your tribe?

Source: book _____   encyclopedia _____   Internet site _____

Native American Bibliography

<u>Book</u>

Title: _____

Author: _____

<u>Encyclopedia</u>

Title: _____

Volume: _____   Page(s): _____

<u>Internet Site</u>

Title: _____

Address: _____

Copyright: _____

Name _____ Famous Person _____

Famous Person Research Bank

When and where was your person born? What kind of family and education did he or she have?

Source: book _____ encyclopedia _____ Internet site _____

What was your person's most important contribution? (Why do we remember him or her?)

Source: book _____ encyclopedia _____ Internet site _____

Famous Person Research Bank (continued)

What are three other interesting things about your person?

Source: book _____   encyclopedia _____   Internet site _____

Famous Person Bibliography

<u>Book</u>

Title: _____

Author: _____

<u>Encyclopedia</u>

Title: _____

Volume: _____   Page(s): _____

<u>Internet Site</u>

Title: _____

Address: _____

Copyright: _____

Using the Index

Research Skills: To use pictures and print to gather information and alphabetical order and key words to locate information. To interpret information using an index. To use an almanac to locate information and summarize and organize by taking notes or outlining.

Grades: 3–5

Purpose: To use an index to answer 10 questions and bold type to locate illustrations.

Prerequisite Skills: Ability to organize and find things in alphabetical order (see Sticks and Stones on page 9).

Format: Group Activity

Materials:

- Copies of an index page. The new True Book series from Children's Press has excellent single page indexes. The questions in this activity are based on the index in Larry Dane Brimner's book, *Bees.* You might want to laminate the index worksheet pages so they won't be written on.

- index worksheet (see page 46)

- pencil and crayon for each person

- free books or other prizes *(optional)*

Prepare in Advance: Make a transparency of the index page. Photocopy the worksheet on page 46 for your students. If you like, reduce the page to fit four per page—using a smaller sheet doesn't seem as much like "doing a worksheet." Cut the question sheets apart. Sharpen the pencils and set them out with the crayons.

Activity Directions:

1. Have a volunteer who feels comfortable with the index come to the front of the class and demonstrate how to use it. Select a second volunteer who is also willing to come up front for a demonstration.

2. Tell the two students that they are going to have an Information Race. Give one student a copy of the index for a short nonfiction book. The other student can use the book, but not the index. Ask them three or four questions and have them call out the page number where they can find the answer.

3. Of course the student with the index will win the race, and either the sympathetic audience or the frustrated non-index user will complain that it's not fair. The point of using an index will have been made without any further explanation needed.

4. Give each student a copy of the index (tell them not to write on it), a question sheet, a pencil and a crayon to use for checking. Do the first one or two questions together. Circle the key word in the question, then locate the page number in the index. The object is not to find the answer, but to locate the pages that could tell the answer. Then have the students work independently. When the students are finished, they should turn over their paper and draw a related picture that you suggest.

5. When everyone is done, collect the pencils. Use the crayons to check the answers together, explaining any answers where necessary. Collect the papers and keep the ones that attempted an illustration in a separate pile. Use the illustrated papers to have a drawing for prizes. I like to do this to reward extra effort. A student may not think he or she is a great artist, but it's a plus if the student tried. Give the papers to their teacher to use for a grade.

Worksheet Answers:

1. 13	6. 24
2. 16–17	7. 30, 32
3. 7	8. 17, 20, 21, 24
4. 35	9. 22
5. 37	10. illustrations or pictures

Index Questions

Materials:

- multiple copies of a new True Book or other easy nonfiction book with a single page index for each student (I used Larry Dane Brimner's book *Bees*.)

- blank paper

- pencils

Prepare in Advance: Collect books for students to use.

Activity Directions:

Have the students use the index in their book to write questions. Students should be sure to include one or two illustration questions and a question about a person. It may be necessary to use the index to find the topic and read about it before writing a question. The answers should be provided on the back. These sheets can be used as additional activity sheets for students in other classes.

Resources

Book:

Library Centers: Teaching Information Literacy, Skills and Processes, K–6 by Judith A. Sykes. Greenwood, 1997.

Web sites:

eLibrary Reference Desk
ask.elibrary.com/refdesk.asp?refid=ency_misc

Encarta Encyclopedia
encarta.msn.com

Enchanted Learning
www.enchantedlearning.com

Encyclopedia.com
www.encyclopedia.com

World Book Encyclopedia
www2.worldbook.com

Name _____   Teacher _____

Index Worksheet

Bees by Larry Dane Brimner

Using the book, *Bees,* write the answers to the following questions. There may be more than one page number for the answer.

1. I know bees have multiple eyes like flies do. Which page shows me what they look like?

   _____

2. Which page tells me that only female bees have a stinger?

   _____

3. How many pages give information about the queen bee?

   _____

4. Which page tells me how bees communicate by dancing?

   _____

5. Which page tells me about Warwick Kerr and what he has to do with bees?

   _____

6. Which page tells me how often bees mate?

   _____

7. Which page tells me if bees make a cocoon or a chrysalis?

   _____

8. Which page tells me what the job of a drone bee is?

   _____

9. Which page tells me how bees make their honeycomb?

   _____

10. What do the page numbers in **boldface** type mean?

    _____

Dictionary Go Fish

Research Skills: To use print to gather information and alphabetical order to locate information. To use a strategy to locate answers, guide words to locate definitions and a dictionary to locate answers to questions.

Grades: K–5 (use grade-level appropriate dictionaries and questions)

Purpose: To learn to use "thirds" to locate words quickly and to use the dictionary to find words, definitions and parts of speech.

Prerequisite Skills: Ability to use alphabetical order (see Sticks and Stones on page 9) and a familiarity with the dictionary, guide words and thirds.

Format: Class Game

Materials:

- 24 tagboard fish for each level (more if class size warrants)

- 24 paper clips

- 2 or 3 dowels

- 2 or 3 magnets

- string

- an appropriate dictionary for each team and each level

- dictionary words (see pages 50–51)

- basket for each team

- chalkboard or chart tablet

Prepare in Advance: Photocopy a class set of fish from the pattern on page 52. Cut them out, then label each one. For Level One, write a grade level word on each fish. For Levels Two and Three, number the fish for use with any numbered list. Laminate the fish. Clip a paper clip to each fish's mouth. Cut a piece of string for the fishing line. The string should be long enough to reach the floor from the child's waist. Attach a magnet to one end, then tie the other end to one end of the dowel. Repeat for the other fishing poles.

Activity Directions:

1. Divide the class into two or three teams.

2. Spread the fish on the floor between the teams in the "pond." All of the fish should be number side down.

3. **LEVEL ONE:** A student "catches" a fish, reads the word aloud and looks it up. This can be done with the help of a partner if desired. The student gives the page number that the word is on. If the student is correct, the fish goes into the team's basket. If the student answers incorrectly, the fish goes back into the "pond" to live another day.

LEVEL TWO: A student "catches" a fish and reads the number aloud. Write the corresponding word on the chalkboard or chart tablet. Then the student looks up the word. A partner can help if desired. Then the student reads the definition that matches the number you specify. If the student reads the correct definition, the fish goes into the team's basket. If it is not the correct definition, the fish goes back into the "pond."

LEVEL THREE: A student "catches" a fish, reads the number aloud, sees you write the word on the chalkboard or chart tablet, then looks it up. This can be done with the help of a partner if desired. Randomly ask the student one of three questions:

a. How many syllables does the word have?
b. What part of speech is the word?
c. What is the meaning given for definition number_____?

If the student answers correctly, the fish goes into the team's basket. If incorrect, the fish goes back into the "pond."

4. At the end of the game, add up the fish in each basket. The team with the most fish wins.

Dictionary Dive

Materials:

- class set of dictionaries

- 3 large cards, chalkboard or whiteboard

Prepare in Advance: On the cards, write the letters A–G, H–O, P–Z. Hang them where students can refer to them.

Activity Directions:

1. The object of this lesson is to get the students to start in the correct third of the dictionary when looking up a word, rather than always starting at the beginning of the book.

2. Use the cards to point out the thirds of the dictionary. When you call a word, all of the students get to open their dictionaries ONE time, then put their hands in their lap. The students earn a point if they are in the correct third of the dictionary. They earn two points if they are in the correct letter and three points if they get the exact page.

3. Before play, divide the students into teams. Call out a word. Give time for all to open dictionaries and determine score. Ask the students to raise their fingers for the points they earned. If they opened to the wrong third, they shouldn't raise their hand at all. Add the points for each team and record. Repeat as often as there is time. Students will become more skillful with practice.

Resources

Dictionaries:

The American Heritage Children's Dictionary by Editors of the American Heritage Dictionaries. Houghton Mifflin, 1998.

The American Heritage First Dictionary by Kaethe Ellis. Houghton Mifflin, 1998.

The DK Children's Illustrated Dictionary by John McIlwain. DK Publishing, 1994.

The Kingfisher Illustrated Children's Dictionary by John Grisewood. Houghton Mifflin, 1994.

MacMillan Dictionary for Children by Robert B. Costello (Editor). Simon & Schuster, 2001.

The McGraw-Hill Children's Dictionary by Vincent Douglas. McGraw-Hill, 2002.

Merriam-Webster's Elementary Dictionary. Merriam-Webster Inc., 2000.

Merriam-Webster's Intermediate Dictionary. Merriam-Webster Inc., 1994.

Scholastic Children's Dictionary. Scholastic, 2002.

Webster's New World Children's Dictionary by Michael Agnes. John Wiley & Sons, Inc., 1999.

Book:

Library Centers: Teaching Information Literacy, Skills and Processes, K–6 by Judith A. Sykes. Greenwood, 1997.

Web sites:

Little Explorers Picture Dictionary
www.littleexplorers.com/Dictionary.html
Click a letter to see related words, many of them connected to carefully selected, kid-friendly sites. Many are suitable for pre-readers.

Merriam-Webster Online Language Center
www.m-w.com/netdict.htm
Includes Collegiate Dictionary, Collegiate Thesaurus and Merriam-Webster Unabridged Dictionary.

Merriam-Webster Word Central
www.wordcentral.com

Sample Dictionary Words

LEVEL ONE: Write a list of 24 words from *The American Heritage First Dictionary* or other beginning dictionary. Make an answer key consisting of the word and its page number.

LEVEL TWO: List of 24 words from *Merriam-Webster's Elementary Dictionary*. Samples are provided below.

Word	Definition No.	Definition
1. abide	3	to live in a place; dwell
2. ability	1	power to do something
3. brilliant	3	very smart or clever
4. carry	8	to sing in correct pitch
5. convey	3	impart or communicate
6. double	4	folded in two
7. engine	3	locomotive
8. enter	3	to become a member
9. follow	7	to keep one's eyes or attention on
10. handy	2	easy to use or manage
11. horn	6	a brass musical instrument
12. humanity	1	kindness
13. incubate	1	to sit upon eggs to hatch them by warmth
14. meringue	1	a mixture of beaten white of egg and sugar
15. navy	3	a dark blue
16. nervy	1	showing calm courage
17. rugged	3	strong
18. shirt	2	undershirt
19. splendor	1	great brightness
20. springy	1	elastic
21. transit	4	a surveyor's instrument for measuring angles
22. vulgar	2	having poor taste or manners
23. waterfowl	1	a bird that is found in or near water
24. whence	2	from or out of which

LEVEL THREE: List of 24 words from *Merriam-Webster's Intermediate Dictionary*. Copy the word and the number of the specified definition onto the fish. Samples are provided below.

Word	Syllables	Part of Speech	Definition and Number
1. aright	2	adverb	so as to be correct
2. attrition	3	noun	1—act of wearing down by friction
3. barbarous	3	adjective	2—cruel
4. calculating	4	adjective	2b—scheming
5. captivate	3	verb	to influence or fascinate by charm
6. conductor	3	noun	2—the leader of a musical group
7. cuneiform	4	adjective	2—written with letters shaped like wedges
8. decipher	3	verb	2—to make out the meaning of
9. domain	2	noun	2—an area of influence
10. fibrous	2	adjective	2—tough
11. guttural	3	adjective	1—pronounced in the throat
12. impish	2	adjective	mischievous
13. limpid	2	adjective	perfectly clear, transparent
14. marathon	3	noun	2—a long hard contest
15. millennium	4	noun	2b—a period of great happiness
16. mismanage	3	verb	to manage badly
17. ponderous	3	adjective	1—very heavy
18. properly	3	adverb	2—according to fact
19. restive	2	adjective	1—stubbornly fighting control
20. scythe	1	noun	a tool that has a curved blade
21. shoat	1	noun	a young hog usually less than one year old
22. trapezoid	3	noun	a four sided plane figure
23. vulnerable	4	adjective	2—open to attack or damage
24. yippee	2	interjection	used to express delight

Fish Pattern

The Great Race (Atlas)

Research Skills: To use alphabetical order to locate information, an index to gather information, a compass rose and map coordinates to interpret information and an atlas to locate information and answer questions.

Grades: 3–5

Purpose: To use an atlas index, compass rose and coordinates to locate 10 places worldwide.

Prerequisite Skills: Ability to use an index, latitude and longitude, map symbols and compass rose.

Format: Team Game

Materials:

• a free book or other prize for the top five winning teams (or the number you select)

For each pair of students:

• 10 envelopes

• laminated set of clues (pages 58–59)

• sheet of notebook paper

• atlas

• scenario (page 57)

Prepare in Advance: Photocopy the clues so you have one set for each team. Cut the clues apart, then laminate them. Label the envelopes 1 through 10 and insert the appropriate clue in each. Each team should have a set of envelopes labeled 1 through 10. The envelope sets should be unique by the color of the numbers, color of the envelopes, a rubber stamp or sticker, etc. Locate an atlas for each team. Number 1–10 on the sheets of notebook paper for the answer sheet.

Activity Directions:

This activity is similar to a reality television program called *The Amazing Race*. Over the span of the television show, teams of two follow various clues to locations scattered across the globe. As they reach each point, they retrieve an envelope that contains the clue to the next location. Finally, the first TV team to the last location wins a large monetary prize.

1. Read the scenario to the class. Give each team their first envelope, answer sheet and atlas.

2. Designate a spot for the Rendezvous Point. This is where the students get their answers checked and receive their next envelope.

3. On "GO!" students open the first envelope, read the clue and search for the answer in their atlas. They record the answer, return the question to the envelope and quickly bring their answer sheet and envelope to the Rendezvous Point to be checked.

4. If the answer is correct, initial it, take the envelope and give out the next one. If the answer is incorrect, send the team back to their atlas, perhaps with a hint.

5. The teams hurry back to their seats and repeat the activity, returning the envelope each time.

6. When the time is up, prizes are awarded to all who finished or to those who completed the most answers. We give away free paperbacks for such a difficult effort.

The Great Race Answers
(From *Rand McNally Quick Reference World Atlas*)

1. France / C4 / p. 30

2. Paris / C4 / p. 30

3. Algeria / E4 / p. 30 or D7 / p. 42

4. Nigeria / G8 / p. 42

5. Uruguay / C5 / p. 21

6. Brazil / D8 / p. 23

7. China / D10 / p. 35

8. Russia / pages 32–33

9. Aral'sk / Kazakhstan / H9 / p. 32

10. Memphis, Tennessee / p. 9

Where in the World am I?

Materials:

- tongue depressors

- large coffee can

- a world map for each pair of students

- pencil and paper for each team

Prepare in Advance: Locate 25 points on a world map and write their coordinates on the tongue depressors. At the same time, create an answer key by recording the location next to the coordinates. Number the tongue depressors from 1–25 and place them in a large can so the numbers can be seen. Photocopy a world map for each team. Photocopy an answer key for each checker.

Activity Directions:

1. Have the students pair up. Each team takes a turn coming up to get a tongue depressor. At their seat, they read the coordinates, look them up on the map and record the stick number and the answer.

2. The teams bring their answers to be checked, draw another stick, record the answer and repeat. Those with the most correct answers at the end of class may win a small prize.

Resources

Atlases:

Atlas of World Facts by Robert Neumiller. Creative Education, 2001.

Children's Atlas of the World by Philip Steele. Franklin Watts, 2000.

Dorling Kindersley Children's Atlas. DK Publishing, 2000.

Encyclopedia of World Geography with Complete World Atlas: Internet-Linked by Gillian Doherty. EDCP, 2002.

My First Atlas. Nicholas Harris. Hammond, 2000.

National Geographic Our World: A Child's First Picture Atlas. National Geographic Society, 2000.

Rand McNally Quick Reference World Atlas. Rand McNally, 2001.

The Reader's Digest Children's Atlas of the World by Colin Sale. Reader's Digest Children's Publishing, Inc., 2000.

Young Learner's U.S. and World Atlas. McGraw-Hill Children's Pub., 2000.

Books:

Great Map Mysteries: 18 Stories and Maps to Build Map and Geography Skills by Susan Julio. Scholastic, 1997.

Information Literacy Toolkit: Grades Kindergarten–6 by Jenny Ryan and Steph Capra. ALA Editions, 2001.

Web sites:

Grid Club
www.gridclub.com/look_it_up/index.shtml
Includes dictionary, thesaurus, atlas and Fact Gadget.

National Geographic Maps and Geography
www.nationalgeographic.com/resources/ngo/maps
Click on the Table of Contents for the MapMachine.

National Geographic Xpeditions
www.nationalgeographic.com/xpeditions
Includes black-and-white maps for printing, lesson plans and student activities and an Interactive Learning Museum.

Quick Maps
www.theodora.com/maps/abc_world_maps.html
This is a good source of maps, including coloring maps for each continent.

The Great Race Scenario

Congratulations! You have been chosen from among thousands of contestants to form one of the lucky teams that will travel the globe. As team members of the Great Race, you will have many exciting adventures as you criss-cross the globe—traveling across countries, mountains and rivers and relying on the natives for help.

You will travel the world attempting to gather clues to each of your destinations. The teams to arrive at the final destination within the time limit will be the grand prize winners. Prizes are:

_____

Each team will begin their trip with the supplies of a pencil, answer sheet, atlas and clue envelope.

Listen for my "GO" before you open your envelope. Does everyone have a pencil? A paper? The first envelope? An atlas?

Ready, set, go!

The Great Race Clues

(Answers from *Rand McNally Quick Reference World Atlas*, 2001.)

Envelope 1

To begin the trip, you will leave the port of **Galveston, Texas** on board the ship *Queen Elizabeth II.* You will land at the port of **Le Havre** in _____.

Coordinates _____ page _____.

Envelope 2

After a dinner of fine French cuisine in Le Havre, you will board a lovely houseboat for a leisurely trip down the Seine River to the **French capital city** of _____.

Coordinates _____ page _____.

Envelope 3

Waste no time getting to the Charles de Gaulle Airport in Paris, where you will fly **directly south** across the Mediterranean Sea to the **African country** of _____.

Coordinates _____ page _____.

Envelope 4

Feast on stuffed dates, couscous and baked lamb, because you will need your strength to get **across the Sahara Desert** to the city of **Kano** in _____.

Coordinates _____ page _____.

Envelope 5

Get help from the natives who, though they don't speak English, are very friendly. Purchase an airline ticket to **Montevideo** in the country of _____.

Coordinates _____ page _____.

Envelope 6

Speaking Spanish will help you in Uruguay, but not where you're going next. You need to find guides to take you down the **longest river** in the world, the **Amazon River**. It is in _____.
Coordinates _____ page _____.

Envelope 7

Use your money well, because now you need to buy a ticket to the **land of the Great Wall**, an ancient wonder built in

_____.

Coordinates _____ page _____.

Envelope 8

A rickshaw will come to your hotel to carry you to the airport for your trip to the **largest country** in the world. It is **north of China**. It is so big it covers two pages. The country is _____
pages_____.

Envelope 9

Buy a train ticket across Russia to the **northern city** on the **Aral Sea**. This city is called _____ in the
country of _____
Coordinates _____ page _____.

Envelope 10

A free book and a relaxing limousine ride await you if you are fast enough to get home first. Both are waiting for you in the **United States**, at the coordinates 90 degrees W and 35 degrees N. What city and state is this? _____

Taming Tired Tales

(Thesaurus)

Research Skills: To use alphabetical order to locate information, an index and guide words to locate synonyms and a thesaurus to enliven writing. To learn to acquire information from an on-line thesaurus.

Grades: 3–5

Purpose: To use the thesaurus to add interest and color to writing.

Prerequisite Skills: Ability to locate things alphabetically (see Sticks and Stones on page 9). Familiarity with the format of the thesaurus and previous practice with finding synonyms in the thesaurus.

Format: Task Cards

Materials:

- laminated task cards (pages 63–66) and photocopies for students

- thesauri

- transparencies of each card to show corrections

Prepare in Advance: Photocopy pages 63–66 on to card stock. Photocopy the cards so that each student has one card to work on. (You may want to have students work in pairs. If you want to shorten correction time, give each student a copy of the same card.) Make a transparency of each card to show the corrections.

Activity Directions:

1. Distribute the photocopied task cards to the students. Have the students name some of the tired and overworked verbs and adjectives on the cards. Ask them to underline every adjective and verb.

2. Have the students use a thesaurus to replace as many dull adjectives and verbs as they can in the allotted time.

3. After the time is up, put up the transparency of each card. Have the students tell you which words are tired (highlight them as they are named). Then have the students tell you which synonyms they used instead.

S·T·R·E·T·C·H·Y ACTIVITY

Thesaurus Triumph

Materials:

- copy of Thesaurus Triumph puzzle for each child (see page 67)

- transparency of puzzle

- computer workstations

Prepare in Advance: Photocopy a puzzle for each child and prepare the transparency. Bookmark the Merriam-Webster Thesaurus site on all student workstations (www.m-w.com/thesaurus.htm).

Activity Directions:

1. Have students open the bookmarked thesaurus Internet site.

2. Distribute the puzzles and work through the first one with the students, showing them how to type in the search term ("happiness") and then read the synonyms and related words to find one that fits the number of squares in the answer. Remind the students that after finding the results for each search, they should use the thesaurus search box to the left. Warn them to be careful not to click on any of the surrounding ads, some of them contain misleading search boxes.

3. A few minutes before the time is up, check the puzzle answers together using the transparency. Write them in as you answer each clue.

Thesaurus Triumph Answers:

Across	Down
2. bliss	1. petite
3. immense	4. sky-high
5. scrawny	5. stubby
7. obese	6. melancholy
9. homely	8. lovely

Resources

Thesauri:

The American Heritage Children's Thesaurus by Paul Hellweg. Houghton Mifflin, 1997.

The Harcourt Brace Student Thesaurus by Christopher Morris. Harcourt, 1991.

The Kingfisher Illustrated Thesaurus by George Beal. Houghton Mifflin, 1996.

Roget's Children's Thesaurus. Harper San Francisco, 1997.

Scholastic Children's Thesaurus by John K. Bollard. Scholastic, 1998.

Simon & Schuster Thesaurus for Children by Jonathan P. Latimer and Karen Stray Nolting. Simon & Schuster, 2001.

Young Learner's Thesaurus with Illustrations. McGraw-Hill, 2001.

Book:

Teaching Library Skills in Grades K through 6: A How-to-Do-It Manual by Catharyn Roach and JoAnne Moore. Neal-Schuman Publishers, 1993.

Web site:

Thesaurus.com
www.thesaurus.com
Includes other resources for writers.

Task Cards for Taming Tired Tales

Card 1

Directions: Use a thesaurus to change at least three of these tired adjectives or verbs to something more interesting. Write the new word in the space above the old word.

A family reunion can be a lot of fun. There will be lots of food, lots of cousins

and lots of games. The best weather is a sunny day, when you can play outside.

Uncles and aunts talk a lot, and boys run races. The cakes and pies look very good

and the barbecue smells good, too. I am very happy that it is coming up soon.

Card 2

Directions: Use a thesaurus to change at least three of these tired adjectives or verbs to something more interesting. Write the new word in the space above the old word.

There are lots of kinds of dogs that make good pets. Some are good at watch-

ing. Some can run fast. Some are very noisy. There are big dogs, little dogs and

even some middle-sized dogs. Some have soft fur and some have rough fur. But

dogs make good friends that can make a child feel happy and safe.

Card 3

Directions: Use a thesaurus to change at least three of these tired adjectives or verbs to something more interesting. Write the new word in the space above the old word.

A train trip to Vancouver, Canada, can be fun. The tracks run right along the edge of Puget Sound. The scenery of the water is pretty and fun to look at. The big windows give the train riders a good look. Good meals are served in the dining car. You can get hot sandwiches and cold drinks. Riding the train is fun!

Card 4

Directions: Use a thesaurus to change at least three of these tired adjectives or verbs to something more interesting. Write the new word in the space above the old word.

Shopping for school can be hard. There are so many choices to make. Should we get baggy jeans or tight jeans? Should we buy dark clothes that might be too hot or light clothes that might be too cool? And what if I grow? Will my clothes be too small before the year is over? I hope my clothes don't look strange.

Card 5

Directions: Use a thesaurus to change at least three of these tired adjectives or verbs to something more interesting. Write the new word in the space above the old word.

I'm feeling sad because our baseball game is going to be canceled. The sky is dark and lightning is flashing white. Next there will be big drops of rain and then the ground will get wet. If it rains too long, I know my coach will call off our most important game. I really feel bad about not getting to play today.

Card 6

Directions: Use a thesaurus to change at least three of these tired adjectives or verbs to something more interesting. Write the new word in the space above the old word.

Don't you dislike being sick? Your stomach hurts, your head hurts, you feel bad all over. You are sad because you can't play outside, can't do anything fun with your friends. Even food tastes bad, and you have to eat bad things like chicken noodle soup, ginger ale and crackers. I am sick of being sick!

Card 7

Directions: Use a thesaurus to change at least three of these tired adjectives or verbs to something more interesting. Write the new word in the space above the old word.

Prince Charming was tired of looking for the girl who owned the small glass slipper. He had been to every house in the kingdom, big or small. Not everyone had been happy to see him. Some even yelled or chased him from their house. Maybe he should just stop trying and go back to his lonely castle for some rest.

Card 8

Directions: Use a thesaurus to change at least three of these tired adjectives or verbs to something more interesting. Write the new word in the space above the old word.

Chili is a recipe that has been around for a long time. Cowboys made it by throwing in whatever leftover meat and vegetables they had, some tomatoes and especially spices. Good chili makes your eyes water and your nose run. The taste hides the plain leftovers so you think you're getting a new meal.

Card 9

Directions: Use a thesaurus to change at least three of these tired adjectives or verbs to something more interesting. Write the new word in the space above the old word.

Growing up is hard for a baby Ridley turtle. Its mother lays her eggs in the sand at night. When the eggs hatch, the babies must go to the sea. While they are trying to get to the water, their enemies catch many of them to eat. Once they are safe in the water, they have more enemies waiting to make a snack of them.

Card 10

Directions: Use a thesaurus to change at least three of these tired adjectives or verbs to something more interesting. Write the new word in the space above the old word.

People have been wearing precious stones as jewelry for years. The emerald is very pretty and green. Diamonds are white and shiny. Pearls are round and pretty and made by oysters. Rubies can be dark red or light red. Jade comes in shades of green. Turquoise comes in shades of blue. All make nice jewelry.

Thesaurus Triumph Crossword Puzzle

Use the thesaurus to find synonyms for the words below. Then fill in the puzzle.

Across

2. happiness
3. large
5. skinny
7. fat
9. ugly

Down

1. small
4. tall
5. short (adj.)
6. sadness
8. pretty (adj.)

Almanac Jeopardy

Research Skills: To use pictures and print to gather information, alphabetical order to locate answers; a strategy to form questions and locate answers; and guide words and indexes to locate needed information. To interpret information using pictures, charts or graphs and to use an almanac to locate information. To acquire information from on-line or CD-ROM resources.

Grades: 3–5

Purpose: To practice using almanacs to find answers to interesting questions.

Prerequisite Skills: Familiarity with the almanac and how to locate a topic, isolate the page and find the answer.

Format: Class Game

Materials:

* Jeopardy questions from pages 71–73 (from *The World Almanac and Book of Facts 2003*)

* transparent plastic disks or pennies for covers

* answer keys (see page 74) and score board

* class set of *The World Almanac and Book of Facts 2003* (or most current version you have)

* paper and pencil for each student

* scoreboard

* laminated class set of game boards

Prepare in Advance: Make transparencies of the game boards on pages 71–73. Photocopy a class set of the game boards and an answer key. Laminate the game boards. Set up the overhead and the game covers or pennies and prepare the scoreboard.

Activity Directions:

1. Divide the class into two teams. Give each student an almanac, paper and a pencil. Hand out a game board to each student. Each team member takes three questions to look up. Allow eight minutes for the teams to look up the answers and write them down on their answer sheet not the game board. Tell them to be sure to write the topic and the amount of money next to each answer.

2. After the time is up, begin the game by calling on someone from the first team to select a category and an amount.

3. Read the question aloud. After conferring with one another, students on both teams raise their hands to answer. Whichever team has two hands raised first gets to answer.

4. If the student's answer is correct, add that amount to the team score. That student calls out another topic and amount. If the answer is incorrect, that amount of money is deducted from the team score (you may have negative amounts at times during the game) and the question reverts to the other team.

5. The team with the most money at the end of the game wins.

Almanac Scavenge

Materials:

- CD-ROM version of an almanac or bookmarked site on workstations

- strips of paper and pencil for each student

- laminated question sheet for each student pair (see page 75)

- copy of answer key on page 76 (Answers are supplied by "World Almanac for Kids," www.worldalmanacforkids.com.)

Prepare in Advance: Photocopy and laminate the questions sheets. Number 1–10 on each paper strip. Then sharpen the pencils and load the CD-ROM almanac or bookmark the almanac site on the workstations.

Activity Directions:

1. Use the CD-ROM or bookmarked on-line almanac to answer the questions at the computers.

2. The students should write their answers on the strip of paper.

3. Five minutes before the end of class, go over the answers, allowing students to check their own work. (The answer key supplies the search path in case students need assistance as they work.)

Resources

Fact Books:

Book of Amazing Facts: A Children's Guide to the World. Reader's Digest, 2000.

The Kingfisher Facts and Records Book by Matthew Turner. Houghton Mifflin, 2000.

The World Almanac for Kids 2003. Griffin, 2002.

Book:

Can You Find It? 25 Library Scavenger Hunts to Sharpen Your Research Skills by Randall J. McCutcheon and Pamela Espeland. Free Spirit Publishing, 1991.

Web sites:

Fact Monster from Information Please
www.factmonster.com
Includes links to Infoplease Atlas, Fact Monster Dictionary, Fact Monster Almanac, and 57,000 articles from Columbia Encyclopedia, Sixth Edition.

Farmer's Almanac
www.farmersalmanac.com

World Fact Almanac
www.odci.gov/cia/publications/factbook

Almanac Jeopardy

Game 1
Thumb Index

Astronomy and Calendar	States of the U.S.	Nations of the World
10 What is the average temperature of Venus?	**10** What is Montana's state nickname?	**10** Which country has a flag that is a single color?
20 On what date will there be a total solar eclipse in 2010?	**20** What is the state motto of Texas?	**20** What is the life expectancy for a male in the United States?
30 What is the Zodiac sign, in English, for Libra?	**30** What is the total area of Massachusetts?	**30** What is the capital of New Zealand?

Almanac Jeopardy

Game 2
Quick Reference Index

Sports	Measurements	Animals
10 Who won Super Bowl XXXIII?	**10** How long is the Nile River?	**10** How fast can a chicken run?
20 Who was the winner of the Indianapolis 500 auto race in 1999?	**20** How many kilograms are in a metric ton?	**20** What is the name of a young swan?
30 Where will the Winter Olympics be held in 2006?	**30** Which is the highest mountain in Africa?	**30** What is the number one dog in American Kennel Club registrations?

Almanac Jeopardy

Game 3
General Index

Stray Facts	Famous People	Transportation
10 What is the zip code for Dallas?	**10** When is the birthday of Britney Spears?	**10** Which world airport has the most passenger traffic?
20 What is the modern birthstone for November?	**20** Who was our 19th president?	**20** What is the Web site for Amtrak railroad?
30 How many zeroes are in an octillion?	**30** What was the title of the best-selling fiction book in 2001?	**30** What ship was sunk on May 7, 1915?

Stretchy Library Lessons: Research Skills

Almanac Jeopardy Answer Key

Note: If you are using an almanac other than The World Almanac and Book of Facts 2003, *you will need to check the answers and revise as necessary.*

Game 1—Thumb Index

Astronomy and Calendar

10—What is the average temperature of Venus? *(867 degrees F)*
20—On what date will there be a total solar eclipse in 2010? *(July 11)*
30—What is the Zodiac sign, in English, for Libra? *(the Balance)*

States of the U.S.

10—What is Montana's state nickname? *(Treasure State)*
20—What is the state motto of Texas? *(Friendship)*
30—What is the total area of Massachusetts? *(10,555 square miles)*

Nations of the World

10—Which country has a flag that is a single color? *(Libya)*
20—What is the life expectancy for a male in the United States? *(74.5 years)*
30—What is the capital of New Zealand? *(Wellington)*

Game 2—Quick Reference Index

Sports

10—Who won Super Bowl XXXIII? *(Denver Broncos)*
20—Who was the winner of the Indianapolis 500 auto race in 1999? *(Kenny Brack)*
30—Where will the Winter Olympics be held in 2006? *(Turin, Italy)*

Measurements

10—How long is the Nile River? *(4,160 miles)*
20—How many kilograms are in a metric ton? *(1,000)*
30—Which is the highest mountain in Africa? *(Kilimanjaro, 19,340 feet)*

Animals

10—How fast can a chicken run? *(9 mph)*
20—What is the name of a young swan? *(cygnet)*
30—What is the number one dog in American Kennel Club Registrations? *(Labrador Retriever)*

Game 3—General Index

Stray Facts

10—What is the zip code for Dallas? *(75221)*
20—What is the modern birthstone for November? *(topaz)*
30—How many zeroes are there in an octillion? *(27)*

Famous People

10—When is the birthday of Britney Spears? *(December 2, 1981)*
20—Who was our 19th president? *(Rutherford B. Hayes)*
30—What was the title of the best-selling fiction book in 2001? *(Desecration)*

Transportation

10—Which world airport has the most passenger traffic? *(Heathrow in London)*
20—What is the Web site for Amtrak railroad? *(www.amtrak.com)*
30—What ship was sunk on May 7, 1915? *(Lusitania)*

Almanac Scavenge Questions

1. What are three animals that live in polar regions?

2. Who invented the word processor?

3. What kind of currency is used in Japan?

4. When did the first space shuttle enter space and what country was it from?

5. What is the average annual temperature (degrees F) in Boston, MA?

6. What country has the smallest population?

7. In the United States, which religious group is the largest?

8. Where will the Olympic Games be held in summer, 2004?

9. What great explorers traveled the United States in 1804?

10. What famous actor was born October 8, 1970?

Almanac Scavenge Answer Key

1. What are three animals that live in polar regions?
   Animals: Where Animals Live: **(any 3) polar bears, musk oxen, caribou, ermines, arctic foxes, walruses, penguins and Siberian huskies**

2. Who invented the word processor?
   Inventions: Inventions That Help Us Communicate: **International Business Machines (IBM)**

3. What kind of currency is used in Japan?
   Nations: Honduras to Mexico: **yen**

4. When did the first space shuttle enter space and what country was it from?
   Space: Shuttles and Space Stations: **1977, United States**

5. What is the average annual temperature (degrees F) in Boston, MA?
   States: Massachusetts: **51.5 degrees F**

6. What country has the smallest population?
   Population: Smallest Countries: **Vatican City**

7. In the United States, which religious group is the largest?
   Religion: Pie graph on title page: **Protestants**

8. Where will the Olympic Games be held in summer, 2004?
   Sports: The Olympic Games: **Athens**

9. What great explorers traveled the United States in 1804?
   U.S. History Timeline: The New Nation 1783–1900: **Lewis and Clark**

10. What famous actor was born October 8, 1970?
    Historical Birthdays: October 8: **Matt Damon**

Bibliography

Books:

Agnes, Michael. *Webster's New World Children's Dictionary*. John Wiley & Sons, Inc., 1999.

Allen, Christine. *Skills for Life: Information Literacy for Grades K–6*. Linworth, 2002.

Beal, George. *The Kingfisher Illustrated Thesaurus*. Houghton Mifflin, 1996.

Biography for Beginners: Sketches for Early Readers. Issue 2, Winter 2002. Favorable Impressions.

Bollard, John K. *Scholastic Children's Thesaurus*. Scholastic, 1998.

Book of Amazing Facts: A Children's Guide to the World. Reader's Digest, 2000.

Brimner, Larry Dane. *Bees*. Children's Press, 2000.

—. *Cockroaches*. Scholastic Library Publishing, 2000.

Buetter, Barbara MacDonald. *Simple Puppets from Everyday Materials*. Sterling Publishing Company, 1998.

Champlin, Connie. *Storytelling with Puppets*. American Library Association, 1997.

Chester, Jonathan. *The Young Adventurer's Guide to Everest: From Avalanche to Zopkiok*. Ten Speed Press, 2002.

Costello, Robert B. (Editor). *MacMillan Dictionary for Children*. Simon & Schuster, 2001.

Doney, Meryl. *Puppets*. Franklin Watts, 1996.

Dorling Kindersley Children's Atlas. DK Publishing, 2000.

Doherty, Gillian. *Encyclopedia of World Geography with Complete World Atlas: Internet-Linked*. EDCP, 2002.

Douglas, Vincent. *The McGraw-Hill Children's Dictionary*. McGraw-Hill, 2002.

Duncan, Donna and Laura Lockhart. *I-Search, You Search, We All Learn to Research: A How-to-Do-It Manual for Teaching Elementary School Students to Solve Information Problems*. Neal-Schuman Publishers, 2000.

Editors of the American Heritage Dictionaries. *The American Heritage Children's Dictionary*. Houghton Mifflin, 1998.

Eisenberg, Michael B. and Robert E. Berkowitz. *Teaching Information and Technology Skills: The Big 6 in Elementary Schools*. Linworth, 1999.

Ellis, Kaethe. *The American Heritage First Dictionary*. Houghton Mifflin, 1998.

Fleming, Denise. *Alphabet Under Construction*. Henry Holt, 2002.

Grisewood, John. *The Kingfisher Illustrated Children's Dictionary*. Houghton Mifflin, 1994.

Haines, Ken and Gill Harvey. *The Usborne Book of Puppets*. EDCP, 1998.

Harris, Nicholas. *My First Atlas*. Hammond, 2000.

Hellweg, Paul. *The American Heritage Children's Thesaurus*. Houghton Mifflin, 1997.

Henson, Cheryl, et al. *The Muppets Make Puppets!* Workman Publishing Company, 1994.

Holub, Joan. *The Valley of the Golden Mummies*. Penguin Putnam, 2002.

Illustrated Encyclopedia of Wildlife, Vol. 12: The Invertebrates, PT. II. Grey Castle Press, 1990.

James, Elizabeth and Carol Barkin. *How to be School Smart: Super Study Skills*. William Morrow & Co., 1998.

James, Elizabeth and Carol Barkin. *How to Write Super School Reports*. HarperCollins, 1998.

Julio, Susan. *Great Map Mysteries: 18 Stories and Maps to Build Map and Geography Skills*. Scholastic, 1997.

Latimer, Jonathan P. and Karen Stray Nolting. *Simon & Schuster Thesaurus for Children*. Simon & Schuster, 2001.

Lohnes, Marilyn. *Fractured Fairy Tales: Puppet Plays & Patterns*. Upstart Books, 2002.

McCutcheon, Randall J. and Pamela Espeland. *Can You Find It? 25 Library Scavenger Hunts to Sharpen Your Research Skills*. Free Spirit Publishing, 1991.

McIlwain, John. *The DK Children's Illustrated Dictionary*. DK Publishing, 1994.

Merriam-Webster's Elementary Dictionary. Merriam-Webster Inc., 2000.

Merriam-Webster's Intermediate Dictionary. Merriam-Webster Inc., 1994.

Mora, Pat. *The Bakery Lady/La señora de la panadería*. Piñata Books, 2001.

——. *A Birthday Basket for Tia*. Simon & Schuster, 1997.

——. *Pablo's Tree*. Simon & Schuster, 1994.

——. *The Rainbow Tulip*. Penguin Putnam, 2003.

——. *Tomás and the Library Lady*. Bantam Doubleday Dell Books for Young Readers, 2000.

Morris, Christopher. *The Harcourt Brace Student Thesaurus*. Harcourt, 1991.

Moxley, Sheila. *ABCD: An Alphabet Book of Cats and Dogs*. Little, Brown, 2001.

Murray, Beth. *Puppet and Theater Activities: Theatrical Things to Do and Make*. Boyds Mills Press, 1994.

National Geographic Our World: A Child's First Picture Atlas. National Geographic Society, 2000.

Neumiller, Robert. *Atlas of World Facts*. Creative Education, 2001.

Polacco, Patricia. *Mrs. Katz and Tush*. Bantam Doubleday Dell Books for Young Readers, 1994.

Rand McNally Quick Reference World Atlas. Rand McNally, 2001.

Roach, Catharyn and JoAnne Moore. *Teaching Library Skills in Grades K Through 6: A How-to-Do-It Manual*. Neal-Schuman Publishers, 1993.

Roget's Children's Thesaurus. Harper San Francisco, 1997.

Ryan, Jenny and Steph Capra. *Information Literacy Toolkit: Grades Kindergarten–6*. ALA Editions, 2001.

Sale, Colin. *Reader's Digest Children's Atlas of the World*. Reader's Digest Children's Publishing, Inc., 2000.

Scholastic Children's Dictionary. Scholastic, 2002.

Small, Ruth V. and Marilyn P. Arnone. *Turning Kids on to Research: The Power of Motivation*. Greenwood, 2000.

Sneed, Brad. *Picture a Letter*. Penguin Putnam, 2002.

Stanley, Deborah B. *Practical Steps to the Research Process for Elementary School*. Greenwood, 2001.

Steele, Philip. *Children's Atlas of the World*. Franklin Watts, 2000.

Sykes, Judith A. *Library Centers: Teaching Information Literacy, Skills and Processes, K–6*. Greenwood, 1997.

Turner, Matthew. *The Kingfisher Facts and Records Book*. Houghton Mifflin, 2000.

The World Almanac and Book of Facts 2003. World Almanac Books, 2002.

The World Almanac for Kids 2003. Griffin, 2002.

Young Learner's Thesaurus with Illustrations. McGraw-Hill, 2001.

Young Learner's U.S. and World Atlas. McGraw-Hill Children's Pub., 2000.

Web sites:

ABC Order
www.learningplanet.com/act/abcorder.asp

Alphabet Zoo
www.primarygames.com/ABC%20Zoo/start.htm

The Alphabuddies
www.dltk-kids.com/alphabuddies/index.html

Biography.com
www.biography.com

eLibrary Reference Desk
ask.elibrary.com/refdesk.asp?refid=ency_misc

Encarta Encyclopedia
encarta.msn.com

Enchanted Learning
www.enchantedlearning.com

Encyclopedia.com
www.encyclopedia.com

Fact Monster from Information Please
www.factmonster.com

Family Fun: All About Puppets
familyfun.go.com/crafts/buildmodel/special
feature/puppets_crafts_sf/

Farmer's Almanac
www.farmersalmanac.com

Gateway to Library Catalogs
www.loc.gov/z3950

Grid Club
www.gridclub.com/look_it_up/index.shtml

Ideas About Note Taking and Citing Sources
www.big6.com/showarticle.php?id=78

Little Explorers Picture Dictionary
www.littleexplorers.com/Dictionary.html

Merriam-Webster Online Language Center
www.m-w.com/netdict.htm

Merriam-Webster Thesaurus
www.m-w.com/thesaurus.htm

Merriam-Webster Word Central
www.wordcentral.com

National Geographic Maps and Geography
www.nationalgeographic.com/resources/ngo/maps

National Geographic Xpeditions
www.nationalgeographic.com/xpeditions

Puppeteers of America
www.puppeteers.org

Quick Maps
www.theodora.com/maps/abc_world_maps.html

Surfing for ABC's
www.siec.k12.in.us/~west/proj/abc

*Teacher's Guide: Teaching Internet Literacy:
Student Activities*
www.yahooligans.com/tg/activities.html

Thesaurus.com
www.thesaurus.com

World Almanac for Kids
www.worldalmanacforkids.com

World Book Encyclopedia
www2.worldbook.com

World Fact Almanac
www.odci.gov/cia/publications/factbook

*World History and Geography: A Guide for High
School Teachers*
www.studentsfriend.com

Yahooligans Biographies Directory
www.yahooligans.com/school_bell/social_
studies/history/biographies

Yucky Roach World: Roaches Revealed
yucky.kids.discovery.com/flash/roaches